13+ Comprehension: Merchant Taylors' School

Practice Papers & In-Depth Guided Answers

R. P. Davis

Accolade Press

Copyright © 2023 Accolade Tuition Ltd

Published by Accolade Tuition Ltd

71-75 Shelton Street

Covent Garden

London WC2H 9JQ

www.accoladetuition.com

info@accoladetuition.com

The right of R. P. Davis to be identified as the author of this work has been asserted by him in accordance with the Copyright, Designs and Patents Act 1988.

All rights reserved. No part of this book may be reproduced in any form or by any electronic or mechanical means, including information storage and retrieval systems, without written permission from the author, except for the use of brief quotations in a book review.

ISBN 978-1-913988-69-2

FIRST EDITION

1 3 5 7 9 10 8 6 4 2

Introduction

For the Year 9 entry exam at Merchant Taylors' School, students must tackle a comprehension test focused on a prose piece.

Our goal with this guide is to help you familiarise yourself with the kind of questions the exam poses and refine your ability to answer them effectively. We aim to do more than merely expose you to the exam's format. We endeavour to teach you how to deconstruct the questions often found in 13+ comprehension exams, and present you with model answers that meet the examiners' standards. We also offer detailed explanations as to why these model answers succeed in fulfilling the marking criteria, to assist students in reproducing such responses.

How This Book Is Set Out

This book offers four papers, each crafted to emulate the distinct style of the Merchant Taylors' School entrance exams, ensuring comprehensive preparation for any candidate.

For each paper, you will find the extract followed by the questions, enabling students to attempt the paper independently. If the student wishes to tackle one of the papers, we recommend a duration of 30 minutes for completion, which allows students to practice under realistic conditions.

After the questions are displayed in isolation, the same questions are presented again, accompanied by model answers and detailed commentary, providing valuable insights and guidance. There is no prescribed approach to using this guide. Students may work independently or with the support of a parent or tutor. The primary objective is to offer the experience of having an expert tutor readily available for guidance and support.

Exam Tips

Within this book, you will find a good deal of question-specific advice. However, there are a number of more general tips that it is important for any 13+ candidate to keep in mind:

- When reading the extract, don't rush. Some papers even set aside 10 minutes explicitly for reading the paper, and do not allow you to look at the questions until those 10 minutes have elapsed. This does not mean that 10 minutes is always necessary – but keep in mind that every school will expect you to read the passage very carefully.

- Read the questions carefully. It sounds obvious, I know, but you wouldn't believe how many times I have seen bright students lose marks simply because they have misread the question.

- Always write in full sentences, unless you are explicitly told this is not required.

- If you are unhappy with an answer, and feel as though you must write something else, do not cross out your old answer until you have fully finished writing the new one – you may be throwing away precious marks!

- Keep quotes from the text short (unless explicitly told otherwise). As a rule of thumb, try and ensure that your quotes are no more than a sentence long.

- Many 13+ papers give candidates blank lines on which to compose their answers. When these appear, take them seriously: they are guidelines regarding how long the examiners would like your answer to be.

Paper One

In the small Irish town of Drumcliff, two somewhat 'unique' police officers, Sergeant MacBride and Constable Dooley, have been given the daunting task of maintaining the peace and keeping crime at a steady zero. Disturbed by the rising crime rate, they come up with an unorthodox solution.

* * *

If one were to visit the local constabulary workhouse of Drumcliff on a given day when the mists right definitely declined to descend upon the town, one would likely see Sergeant MacBride and Constable Dooley pondering inscrutable truths known only to the keepers of the law. These two diligent guardians of justice often found themselves ensnared in a knot they seemed unable to untangle – a knot woven together by the very threads of law and order, or lack thereof.

"The people, they report crimes, do they not?" mused MacBride one day, eyeglasses perched on a bulbous nose, his hands clasped over a robust stomach, burdened and constantly filled by splendid Irish stew.

"Aye, that they do," answered the more lithe and swift Dooley, nursing a cup of black tea and peering out the window at the town square below, laden with bustling villagers, the heart of Drumcliff beating with a lively rhythm.

"But who do they report them to, lad?" challenged MacBride, his eyes twinkling under bushy brows, like the moon half-hidden in an inky pool.

"To us, of course," replied Dooley, a hint of confusion creeping into his voice, like a timid fox into a coyote's den.

"Aha, precisely my point! So, it stands to reason that if there were to be no one reporting any crimes, then by definition, there would be no crimes at all would there?"

Silence befell the room, punctuated only by the ticking of an ancient clock on the wall, its hands dawdling as if lured by the enticement of the riddle in the air. Dooley turned to his superior, a perplexed furrow etching lines on his forehead, a puzzled silence hanging between them.

"But, Sergeant... Wouldn't that mean..." stammered Dooley, twilight gray eyes round as saucers, slowly recognizing the dangerous edge they were teetering upon.

"Yes," MacBride interjected, understanding lighting his eyes like a midnight bonfire on Saint John's Eve. "Our duty, henceforth, shall be to detain those who report the crimes and not the miscreants. That, lad, will be the end of all crime in Drumcliff!"

And thus, they embarked upon this operation, a scheme peculiar enough to have been conceived in Faerieland itself. Strangely, the villagers complied. Maybe out of fear of becoming criminals themselves, maybe out of curiosity, or maybe out of bored fatigue from the otherwise dreary life, the inhabitants of Drumcliff fell into an unsettling tranquility.

Each day, MacBride and Dooley paced the village, eyes stony with dedication, a hint of madness gnawing at their heels. A cry for help? Charge the caller, not the attacker. The telltale aroma of illegal brew flooding from the cellar of O'Malley's Tavern? Penalise old widow O'Malley for raising the alarm. Reporting became a sin, silence became the law, and before long, the bizarre became the norm.

As the weeks passed, the bewildering silence seeped into the veins of Drumcliff's life. Even as the criminals dwindled, there was stoic silence from the citizens. Crime was now a mere ghost, a gray echo in the bright painting that Drumcliff was slowly becoming. A twisted tranquillity ruled the town. Justice, it seemed, wore not a blindfold but a gag.

Extract from "The Serenade of Silence" by Dermot Callaghan.

QUESTIONS

1. Arrange the following events in order according to when they happened in the extract. Number them from 1 to 5, where 1 is the first event and 5 is the last occurrence. [5]

- MacBride and Dooley patrol the village, enforcing their new rule. ☐
- Dooley recognises the implications of MacBride's suggestion. ☐
- MacBride proposes their duty is to detain those who report crimes. ☐
- Crime becomes a gray echo in the bright painting of Drumcliff. ☐
- MacBride ponders who people report crimes to. ☐

2. Describe the feelings of Constable Dooley when he first understood MacBride's proposed solution to deal with their crime problem (paragraph 8). [4]

3. The author uses a simile to describe MacBride's eyes as 'twinkling under bushy brows, like the moon half-hidden in an inky pool'. What image does this simile create? [4]

4. What do you think the sergeant means when he says, 'Justice, it seemed, wore not a blindfold but a gag'? [4]

_____

_____

_____

_____

_____

_____

_____

_____

5. Choose the correct meaning for the word 'perplexed' found in paragraph 7. [2]

Angry

Confused

Surprised

Rushed

Excited

6. Refer to the final paragraph. How does the author create a sense of a surprisingly serene atmosphere in the town? Use at least two quotes in your answer. [4]

_____
_____
_____
_____
_____
_____
_____

7. In your own words, describe the effect of the new rule on the people of Drumcliff. [4]

_____
_____
_____

8. Think of two words that, in your opinion, best describe Sergeant MacBride's plan in dealing with crime. [4]

8a.

8b.

9. Identify three occasions in the text where the writer generates tension

and suspense around the implementation of the new crime reporting rule. Ensure to give the paragraph numbers for each occasion and explain how it made the text suspenseful. [9]

Example:
_____
_____

Explanation:

_____
_____
_____
_____

Example:
_____
_____

Explanation:

_____
_____
_____
_____

Example:
_____
_____

Explanation:

_____

_____

_____

_____

Merchant Taylors' School

MODEL ANSWERS

1. Arrange the following events in order according to when they happened in the extract. Number them from 1 to 5, where 1 is the first event and 5 is the last occurrence. [5]

The correct order of events is:

1) MacBride ponders who people report crimes to;
2) Dooley recognises the implications of MacBride's suggestion;
3) MacBride proposes their duty is to detain those who report crimes;
4) MacBride and Dooley patrol the village, enforcing their new rule;
5) Crime becomes a gray echo in the bright painting of Drumcliff.

* * *

2. Describe the feelings of Constable Dooley when he first understood MacBride's proposed solution to deal with their crime problem (paragraph 8). [4]

Upon first understanding Sergeant MacBride's radical plan to combat crime, Constable Dooley was taken aback and displayed feelings of shock, bewilderment, and hesitation. His reaction is depicted as a mixture of astonishment and concern, symbolised by his 'twilight gray eyes [becoming] round as saucers' and his speech starting to stammer, demonstrating the overwhelming surprise and nervous apprehension he feels about the unconventional proposal.

* * *

3. The author uses a simile to describe MacBride's eyes as twinkling like 'the moon half-hidden in an inky pool'. What image does this simile create? [4]

This simile projects an image of wisdom mixed with mystical curiosity. The reference to the moon half-hidden creates a picture of partial disclosure or something shrouded in mystery, adding to MacBride's enigmatic persona. The "twinkling" suggests a spirited, perhaps mischievous, intellect, reinforcing MacBride's role as the mastermind of the unorthodox plan. Thus, the simile creates an image of MacBride's cunning and instinctive savvy, imbued with an element of secrecy and charm.

* * *

4. What do you think the sergeant means when he says, 'Justice, it seemed, wore not a blindfold but a gag'? [4]

Sergeant MacBride's statement, 'Justice, it seemed, wore not a blindfold but a gag' is indicative of the altered and paradoxical state of law and order in Drumcliff. While justice is traditionally symbolised as being blindfolded to portray its impartiality, the gag metaphorically signifies the enforced silence imposed on the townsfolk, reflecting the topsy-turvy policing strategy of penalising those who report crimes rather than the perpetrators. Consequently, the usual symbol of fairness in justice is replaced by a symbol of suppression - it's not about not seeing the wrongdoings, but being silenced against speaking out about them.

* * *

5. Choose the correct meaning for the word 'perplexed' found in paragraph 7. [2]

The appropriate meaning for the word 'perplexed' in this context is 'Confused'.

* * *

6. Refer to the final paragraph. How does the author create a sense of a surprisingly serene atmosphere in the town? Use at least two quotes in your answer. [4]

The author skilfully conjures a sense of an unexpectedly serene atmosphere in the extract by deftly joining imagery of tranquillity with circumstances that are ordinarily alarming. For example, the phrase 'twisted tranquillity ruled the town' cleverly juxtaposes peacefulness with the strange suppression strategy, indicating an unusual calm derived from a curious situation. Moreover, the depiction of 'crime... [becoming] a gray echo in the bright painting that Drumcliff was slowly becoming' implies a noticeable reduction in crime, further enhancing the surreal tranquillity despite the oppressive rule in place. The author, therefore, creates a peculiarly serene atmosphere rich with irony and contrary to anticipation.

7. In your own words, describe the effect of the new rule on the people of Drumcliff. [4]

The new rule had a profound, albeit unusual effect on the people of Drumcliff. Fear of being accused of a crime themselves for reporting one, curiosity, or simply boredom, led the villagers to comply with MacBride and Dooley's innovative strategy, hence creating an eerie tranquillity in the village. This unconventional approach resulted in silence being deemed the law and reporting a crime a sin. Consequently, crime significantly diminished, becoming just a mere 'gray echo' in Drumcliff's existence. The town was under a peculiar kind of peace, or 'twisted tranquillity', revealing the drastic transformation of societal norms under the influence of this unorthodox law enforcement strategy.

* * *

8. Think of two words that, in your opinion, best describe Sergeant MacBride's plan in dealing with crime. [4]

8a. Innovative: MacBride's plan is undeniably innovative. By diverging from traditional methods of enforcing law and order and focusing on those who report the crimes rather than the criminals themselves, he introduces a refreshingly unconventional perspective on criminal justice.

8b. Radical: The plan can also be described as radical. It significantly alters the focus of law enforcement from the perpetrator to the informant, prompting a paradigm shift in how crime is perceived and handled in Drumcliff. This drastic shift and its successful implementation underpin the radical nature of the plan.

* * *

9. Identify three occasions in the text where the writer generates tension and suspense around the implementation of the new crime reporting rule. Ensure to give the paragraph numbers for each occasion and explain how it made the text suspenseful. [9]

Example 1: Paragraph 4 - MacBride's pondering.

Explanation: When MacBride begins to question who people report crimes to, the author builds a subtle tension as readers are left musing over where MacBride's line of thinking is leading. His questions and the heavy pause before his revelation create anticipation, building suspense in the narrative.

Example 2: Paragraph 9 - "Yes," MacBride interjected..."

Explanation: Here another wave of suspense is created by MacBride's sudden interception of Dooley's stammering. His confirmation and the unveiling of their new duty infuses understanding but also a hint of an ominous future, leaving readers in suspense as to how such an unconventional plan would work in practice.

Example 3: Paragraph 10- 'Strangely, the villagers complied...'

Explanation: The suspense is heightened as the villagers bewilderingly agree to the new rule. This strange silent acceptance raises questions in the readers' minds about the motives behind their compliance- whether it's out of fear, curiosity or simply monotony. This ambiguity and the anticipation of its consequences add an extraordinary amount of tension to the narrative.

Commentary on Model Answers

Question 1

The first mark for question one is gained by correctly identifying the first event in the extract, which is 'MacBride ponders who people report crimes to'. The second and third marks are awarded for correctly identifying the next two events, 'Dooley recognises the implications of MacBride's suggestion' and 'MacBride proposes their duty is to detain those who report crimes'. The fourth mark comes from correctly identifying the penultimate event, which is 'MacBride and Dooley patrol the village, enforcing their new rule'. Lastly, the fifth mark is scored by correctly identifying the final event, 'Crime becomes a gray echo in the bright painting of Drumcliff'. The order of these events properly captures the sequence given in the extract.

However, there could have been a bit of confusion on whether MacBride proposes their new duty before or after Dooley realises the implications of such a suggestion. The text, however, makes it clear that Dooley's realisation comes just before MacBride articulates their new duty. Hence, this order in the response. Each event is equally important to get the order right, hence each one contributing a mark.

Question 2

The first mark for question two is earned by conveying the shock of Dooley when he initially grasped the unconventional idea proposed by MacBride, indicating his astonishment at the unexpected solution.

The second and third marks are obtained by suggesting bewilderment and hesitation, underlining his inability to immediately accept or refute the proposed plan. By doing so, the response captures the range of emotions experienced by Dooley.

The fourth mark is achieved by depicting the nervous apprehension of Dooley, showing his concern about the potential risks and consequences involved in implementing such an unconventional idea. An alternate approach could have detailed more on the descriptive use of 'twilight gray eyes round as saucers' to illustrate his shocked state, focusing more on the interpretation of this visual image.

Question 3

The first mark for question three is gained by correctly identifying the simile 'the moon half-hidden in an inky pool' used by the author, demonstrating a good understanding of the literary device in context.

The second mark is granted for accurately interpreting the first part of the simile, illustrating how the description of MacBride's eyes as 'twinkling' implies a spirited intellect. This extends the analysis to understand the simile in relation to MacBride's characterisation.

The third mark is secured by focusing on the secretive implication of the 'moon half-hidden', which conveys the mysterious aspect of MacBride's personality, and hence giving depth to the simile's interpretation.

The fourth mark is awarded by linking the simile to MacBride's cunning and inventive nature, recognising the simile's contribution to presenting his character. Another approach could have been to focus on the 'half-hidden' aspect of the moon, exploring how this could symbolise MacBride's partial disclosure of his intentions or his propensity for indirect solutions.

Question 4

The first and second marks for question four are scored by understanding the conventionally accepted symbol of justice as being blindfolded – a portrayal of its impartiality, and how the statement juxtaposes it with a figure of speech that suggests suppression of voices, showing the upside-down aspect of justice in Drumcliff.

The third and fourth marks are secured by extending the interpretation to the context of Drumcliff, pointing out how the suppression of crime reporting has ironically led to a suppression of justice, creating a nuanced understanding of the unusual situation. Alternatively, another approach could have been to explore the consequences of this 'gagged' justice – perhaps linking it with the atmosphere of 'serenity' depicted towards the end of the extract.

Question 5

For question five, the first mark is obtained by identifying 'Confused' as the appropriate meaning of 'perplexed', and the second mark is for justifying the selection of this meaning based on Dooley's response to MacBride's proposal in the extract.

Question 6

The first mark for question six is achieved by correctly identifying two phrases that contribute to outlining the surprisingly serene atmosphere: 'twisted tranquillity ruled the town' and 'crime... [becoming] a gray echo in the bright painting that Drumcliff was slowly becoming'.

The second and third marks are gained by explaining these phrases in relation to their contribution to the unanticipated peacefulness. It demonstrates an understanding of how vocabulary choices can establish a specific mood or atmosphere.

The fourth mark is awarded by proficiently connecting the identified quotes to the larger context of the town's bizarre shift into a suppressed but peaceful state, highlighting the peculiar outcome of the unconventional approach to crime control. An alternative approach could have been to discuss the role of village inhabitants in developing this serene atmosphere.

Question 7:

The first mark for question seven comes from outlining that the villagers complied with the rule. This shows an understanding of how the rule played out in the town when implemented.

The second mark highlights the curious reasons for the villagers' compliance: fear, curiosity, or mere tedium. This observation conveys a deeper understanding of the villagers' motivations and the resulting societal impact.

The third mark attempts to discern how this impacted everyday social norms, describing reporting a crime as "a sin," and silence as "the law." This clear description indicates a thorough comprehension of the rule's disruptive effect on societal norms.

The fourth mark is scored by referencing how crime became a "gray echo" and "twisted tranquillity" ruled the town. The vivid description shows a profound understanding of the narrative and its impacts, capturing the peculiar tranquillity that settled over the town.

Question 8:

The word 'Innovative' is chosen because MacBride's idea diverts from conventional police methods, creating a non-traditional solution to tackle crime. This word earns one mark, as it accurately encapsulates the chief's forward-thinking strategy.

The next word, 'Radical', earns the remaining mark because MacBride's approach is not just innovative, it vastly differs from traditional crime-solving methods, shifting the focus from the criminal to the reporter. This assertion encapsulates the plan's revolutionary nature in challenging societal norms and judicial expectations.

Question 9:

The first three of the nine marks are achieved with the first example, that is MacBride's pondering moment and the subtle suspense created. The explanation scores the remaining two marks by elaborating on the suspense created through clever pacing and delivery of MacBride's revelation.

The second set of three marks is earned with the second example where the dubious nature and sudden introduction of the new duty to Dooley is pointed out. The remaining two marks are scored by further explaining the resulting suspense in anticipation of how the plan will be implemented.

The final three marks are obtained by pointing out the intrigue and uncertainty raised when the villagers comply with the unconventional rule. The remaining two marks are earned by explaining how this raises even greater suspense, leaving readers questioning the villagers' motivations and anticipating the rule's consequences.

It's important to note that while these responses are robust, the marks could have been earned with different but equally valid examples and explanations from the text. Always encourage students to justify their responses well, even if their chosen examples vary from the model.

Paper Two

In this extract, set in the early 19th century, the protagonist has recently been hired as a governess for a wealthy family in rural England.

* * *

The family's youngest, a boy of three, a cherubic vision of blond curls and rosy cheeks, was adept at keeping me on my toes. Precocious and unmanageably adventurous, the little tyke caused me great alarm more often than I believe is common for his tender age. This very day, while engaged in our customary outing upon the expansive grounds, I caught sight of a disquieting development down the narrow trail that separated the house from the stables.

From the corner of my eye, I spotted the thunderous approach of a horse, a satin beast of tremendous size and untamed ferocity, far too powerful for the tranquil meanderings of a child. The boy, in his innocent naïveté, saw only a familiar creature, and thus embarked on a wilful sprint towards him with arms outstretched. My heart seemed to have stalled in my chest as I beheld the scene.

Shrieking of the danger was a futile effort; I knew the thunderous hoofbeats drowned my voice. Each passing moment carved itself into my memory as an agonizing eternity. In that interlude of helpless dread, a new spirit seemed to rise within me; a force not of dread, but of iron courage and an unyielding determination of spirit.

Lastly, eschewing all the natural reflexes that called for self-preservation, I found myself charging forward. The world seemed to narrow down to a single imperative - to reach the boy before the horse did.

At that moment of intense disarray, the mantle of fear evaporated under the searing touch of courage. I could only vaguely register the tearing of fabric as my humble gown protested against my desperate, awkward run and the unbecoming grunts of exertion that escaped my ever gasping lungs.

Deaf to the protests of my thighs and lungs alike, I pushed forward with a fervour crossbred from desperation and resolve.

Then, just as the massive body of the charging horse loomed portentously near, I lunged, seizing the boy by his white lace collar. The world erupted into a grand cacophony as I hit the ground, rolling on the grassy earth with the boy clutched protectively in my arms.

The horse, finding its path blocked, let out a wilful whinny, riding high on its hind legs. I averred then that, had it possessed a wrathful mind, it would have cursed the liberty taken by a lowly governess.

Nightingales traced their melodies amidst the shock-wrought silence that fell upon us then. The boy, frightened but unhurt, sobbed into my shabby frock while onlookers, drawn by the harrowing commotion, appeared, their faces contorted in dismay and relief alike.

Yet when the initial shock waned, replaced by bone-deep exhaustion and a sigh of victory over Death's snare, I found that still within me glowed a warm brazier of courage, untouched and unfazed. It illuminated a part of my soul hitherto unknown.

Within the quiet confines of my heart, I marvelled at this discovery. In the deadly dance with danger, it had been fear and courage which danced the waltz. One leading, then the other. As I slowly stood up, dusting off the blades of grass from my frock, I met the gaze of the onlookers. Their eyes, previously filled with horror, now shone with respect and unmistakable admiration. Whispers of my bravery spread amongst them, and I realized that today's event would not only be a memory etched in my mind but would become a tale passed down in hushed tones among the community. An extraordinary courage born of an ordinary fear. It was a dance whose memory would replay in my mind again, in quieter times and under safer shadows.

I, as the newly found bastion of bravery, would live and recount the tale as neither a boastful narrative nor a disgraceful reminder of panic, but an enduring testament to the human capacity to care, to love, and when circumstances conscript - to display great courage.

13+ Comprehension

Extract from "The Dance of Fear and Courage" by C.L. Brookfield.

QUESTIONS

1. Arrange the following events in the order they occur in the extract. [5]

- The protagonist rescues the boy from the horse. ☐

- The protagonist notices a horse approaching seriously. ☐

- The bystanders arrive. ☐

- The protagonist feels a surge of courage. ☐

- The boy runs towards the horse. ☐

2. Analyse the protagonist's emotions in the second and third paragraph when she realises the danger the boy is in. Use your own words. [4]

_____

_____

3. The writer describes the charging horse as 'a satin beast of tremendous size and untamed ferocity.' What does this metaphor make you envisage? [4]

4. What does the writer imply when she says, 'Within the quiet confines of

my heart, I marvelled at this discovery.'? [4]

5. Select the closest meaning to the word 'portentously' (paragraph 7). [2]

a) menacingly

b) curiously

c) hesitantly

d) loudly

e) happily

6. In paragraph 4, discuss how the writer creates a sense of impending danger. Include two quotes in your answer. [4]

_____
_____
_____
_____
_____
_____
_____
_____

7. In your own words, describe how the protagonist's actions impact the people who witness her bravery. [4]

_____
_____
_____
_____
_____
_____

8. Think of two words that, in your opinion, best describe the protagonist's rush towards the boy. [4]

8a.

8b.

9. Identify three points in the text where the writer makes the moment of the horse's approach thrilling for the reader. Provide the paragraph number and explain for each. [9]

Example:

Explanation:

_____
_____
_____
_____

Example:

_____
_____

Explanation:

_____
_____
_____
_____

Example:

_____
_____

Explanation:

_____
_____
_____

MODEL ANSWERS

1. Arrange the following events in the order they occur in the extract. [5]

a) The protagonist rescues the boy from the horse.

b) The protagonist notices a horse approaching seriously.

c) The bystanders arrive.

d) The protagonist feels a surge of courage.

e) The boy runs towards the horse.

The correct order would be: a) The protagonist notices a horse approaching seriously; b) The boy runs towards the horse; c) The protagonist feels a surge of courage; d) The protagonist rescues the boy from the horse; e) The bystanders arrive.

* * *

2. Analyse the protagonist's emotions in the second and third paragraph when she realises the danger the boy is in. Use your own words. [4]

In the second and third paragraphs, the protagonist initially experiences paralysing fear and anxiety on realising the danger that the boy is in – this is illustrated when she describes her heart as having "stalled" in her chest. However, as the imminent danger continues, she experiences a change; a transformation occurs within her, where her fear gives rise to a formidable courage and resolve. This emotional transition, symbolised by the metaphor of a rising spirit, defines this moment; it speaks to her determination and propels her to override her fear and take the necessary action to protect the boy.

* * *

3. The writer describes the charging horse as 'a satin beast of tremendous size and untamed ferocity.' What does this metaphor make you envisage?
[4]

The metaphor engenders visions of a powerful, imposing creature that is as much frightening as it is majestic. 'Satin' alludes to the sleekness and shine of the horse's coat, invoking an image of stunning beauty, while 'beast' conveys the forceful, animalistic side of the horse. 'Tremendous size' further amplifies the physical threat represented by the horse, and 'untamed ferocity' personifies it as a wild, free-spirited creature indifferent to human codes of conduct. Hence, this metaphor serves to augment the danger presented by the horse, heightening the suspense and tension in the scene.

* * *

4. What does the writer imply when she says, 'Within the quiet confines of my heart, I marvelled at this discovery.'? [4]

The writer, through this statement, implies that the protagonist, within her heart's innermost spaces, is astounded and captivated by her own ability to rise to the occasion, and act bravely and decisively under intense pressure. This 'discovery' represents an introspective moment of self-realisation, where she recognises her capacity for incredible courage, a quality she perhaps had not acknowledged within herself before. It signifies a significant shift in her self-perception: an illuminating revelation of her power and resilience, kindled by the dangerous confrontation with the horse.

* * *

5. Select the closest meaning to the word 'portentously' (paragraph 7). [2]

a) menacingly

b) curiously

c) hesitantly

d) loudly

e) happily

Among the given options, 'menacingly' is the closest in meaning to 'portentously'.

* * *

6. In paragraph 4, discuss how the writer creates a sense of impending danger. Include two quotes in your answer. [4]

In paragraph 4, the sense of impending danger is enhanced through dramatic descriptions and movement. The phrase "world seemed to narrow down to a single imperative - to reach the boy before the horse did" crystallises the protagonist's sole goal and paints a vivid image of her singular, desperate focus, heightening the tension. Further, "esche[wing] all natural reflexes that called for self-preservation" emphasizes the direness of the situation, portraying the threat the horse poses as so great that the protagonist ignores her own safety to save the boy. These descriptions amplify the sense of danger and urgency, making the narrative thrilling and suspenseful.

7. In your own words, describe how the protagonist's actions impact the people who witness her bravery. [4]

The protagonist's courageous actions leave an indelible impact upon the witnesses. They positively impact them, as evidenced by their expressions indicating both relief and admiration. People are drawn by the harrowing clamour of the scene, suggesting the profound effect her boldness has on them. Moreover, her actions serve as a testament to human courage, empathy, love, and an inherent drive to protect. Her bravery enhances their respect for her and transforms the entire incident into an enduring shared memory that will reverberate within their community.

8. Think of two words that, in your opinion, best describe the protagonist's rush towards the boy. [4]

8a. Fearless: Despite the imminent danger posed by the thunderous beast racing towards the child, the protagonist exhibits a stunning absence of fear. She disregards all instincts of self-preservation to ensure the child's safety - a display of exceptional fearlessness which dares to confront death itself.

8b. Gallant: Through a gallant rush to rescue the boy - ignoring her torn gown, her gasping lungs, and the protests of her aching thighs - the protagonist personifies courage. It personifies the very essence of a hero, demonstrating an overwhelming love that compels her to place the child's safety above her own.

9. Identify three points in the text where the writer makes the moment of the horse's approach thrilling for the reader. Provide the paragraph number and explain for each. [9]

Example 1: Paragraph 2 - "...a satin beast of tremendous size and untamed ferocity..."

Explanation: The frightening depiction of the approaching horse as 'a satin beast of tremendous size and untamed ferocity' paints a terrifying image. The contrasting use of 'satin', which is generally associated with delicacy or luxury, adds an unexpected layer to the aggression embodied in 'beast', evoking a sense of thrill and tension in the reader.

Example 2: Paragraph 3 - "Each passing moment carved itself into my memory as an agonising eternity."

Explanation: Through dramatising the stretch of time, tension builds up as the impending threat appears to consume every waking second. It encapsulates the protagonist's terror, and by doing so, Brookfield intensifies the reader's apprehension, creating a thrilling reading experience.

Example 3: Paragraph 8 - "The horse, finding its path blocked, let out a wilful whinny, riding high on its hind legs."

Explanation: The climax culminates at this point, as the protagonist's daring intervention halts the threatening horse. The envisaged image of the horse's frustrated rearing creates a vividly thrilling spectacle, leaving readers in suspense as they contemplate the aftermath of such a dramatic collision of circumstances.

Commentary on Model Answers

Question 1

The first mark for question one is achieved by accurately identifying the first event, 'The protagonist notices a horse approaching seriously'. Marks two and three are secured via correctly identifying the subsequent events, 'The boy runs towards the horse' and 'The protagonist feels a surge of courage'. The fourth and fifth marks are successfully obtained by correctly stating the last two events, 'The protagonist rescues the boy from the horse' and 'The bystanders arrive.' This sequence accurately represents the chronology of events presented in the extract and gains all five possible marks.

Question 2

The first mark in question two is garnered by indicating the protagonist's initial emotions of 'paralysing fear and anxiety'. This demonstrates a keen understanding of the protagonist's emotional state upon realising the imminent danger.

The second mark is earned through mentioning the protagonist's heart having "stalled," which effectively captures her sense of dread and shock. This vivid expression, in her own words, amplifies the intensity of her experience for the reader.

The third mark is achieved by noting her subsequent surge of 'formidable courage and resolve', highlighting the emotional transformation that occurs within her in response to the dangerous situation. This indicates a nuanced understanding of the protagonist's complex emotional journey.

The fourth mark is secured by discussing the metaphor of 'a rising spirit' and how it symbolises the transformation of fear into courage. This provides an insightful exploration of the character's emotional development and the psychological implications of the fraught situation, further demonstrating comprehension of the text.

Question 3

The first mark for question three is secured by elucidating the implications of the term 'satin' in the metaphor. The comprehension answer astutely links the term 'satin' to the sleekness and shine of the horse's coat, which captures an aspect of its majestic beauty.

The second mark is achieved by unraveling the deeper meaning behind the word 'beast'. By drawing attention to the horse's forceful, animalistic side, the answer offers a clear interpretation that captures the dual nature of the horse, blending its beauty with its potent threat.

The acquisition of the third mark is credited to the understanding of the phrases 'tremendous size' and 'untamed ferocity'. The answer successfully captures the sense of danger embodied by the horse, emphasizing its wild and indomitable spirit, indifferent to human norms.

Lastly, the fourth mark is clinched by recognizing the overall role of the metaphor in the narrative. The answer rightly notes that the metaphor significantly amplifies the suspense and tension of the scene. This observation speaks to an in-depth understanding of how linguistic choices can shape and elevate the mood and atmosphere of a passage.

Question 4

The first mark for question four is acquired by correctly understanding that the statement, 'Within the quiet confines of my heart, I marvelled at this discovery', implies a sense of astonishment and self-realisation within the protagonist.

The second mark is achieved by highlighting the protagonist's internal introspection and self-discovery. This is a crucial point since this discovery marks an important moment of character development.

The third mark is garnered by inferring a shift in the protagonist's self-perception, sparked by a life-threatening event. It shows an ability to infer deeper meanings from the text.

The fourth mark is obtained by recognising the transformative effect of danger on the protagonist's perception of herself and her capabilities. This realisation shows a nuanced understanding of character development within the text and contributes to scoring the fourth mark.

Question 5

The first mark for question five is secured by identifying the correct option, 'menacingly' which is closest in meaning to 'portentously'. This choice demonstrates a strong understanding of vocabulary and the ability to map synonyms correctly.

The second mark can be achieved by justifying why 'menacingly' is the correct choice, given that 'portentously' is oft en associated with indicating that something momentous or calamitous is likely to happen. An alternative approach could have been to eliminate other options by explaining why they wouldn't match the context or meaning.

Question 6

The first mark in question six is obtained by quoting appropriate phrases from the paragraph, such as "world seemed to narrow down to a single imperative - to reach the boy before the horse did" and "eschewing all natural reflexes that called for self-preservation." This quotation selection demonstrates an understanding of the text and its components that contribute to creating a sense of impending danger.

The second mark is scored by correctly interpreting the phrases, suggesting an image of determined focus and metaphorically conveying the protagonist's disregard for her own safety in favour of protecting the boy. This observation reinforces the understanding of the sense of urgency and danger in the scene.

The third and fourth marks are scored by analysing the narrative techniques in the text, explaining how these descriptions amplify a sense of impending danger and heighten the narrative's suspense. This clear understanding of how to analyse narrative techniques to uncover meanings and generate effects culminates in securing all four marks.

Question 7

The first mark is achieved in the answer to question seven by indicating that the protagonist's brave actions had a significant effect on the onlookers. This shows comprehension of the impact of the situation on the crowd.

The second mark is achieved by illustrating that the onlookers' expressions of both relief and admiration show the positive impact of the protagonist's actions. This detail further illustrates the readers understanding of the reaction by those witnessing.

For the third mark, the acknowledgement that her bravery serves as a testament to human courage and love demonstrates a deeper analysis of the story beyond its basic narrative. It shows an understanding of underlying themes and more subtle implications.

The fourth mark is achieved by pointing out that the incident becomes a shared memory, giving a sense of the broader social context and the lasting significance of the protagonist's actions.

Question 8

The first mark for question eight is earned with the word 'fearless', which accurately describes the protagonist's daring actions facing imminent danger.

The second mark is secured with the explanation that the protagonist disregards self-preservation, specific textual details that further justify the word choice.

The third mark is achieved with the word 'gallant', which aptly describes the protagonist's heroic action in rescuing the boy.

The fourth and final mark comes from the given explanation, referencing specific details from the text such as the protagonist ignoring her own physical discomfort to save the boy.

Question 9

The first three marks in question nine are earned with the first example and explanation. The phrase chosen is a clear point of thrill in the text, and the explanation analyses the contrast and frightening image to create the thrill for the reader.

The next three marks are achieved with the second chosen quote and explanation. It is an apt choice, depicting the protagonist's dread and the tension created by the approaching horse. The explanation refers back to the metaphor in the text, outlining its contribution to the thrilling narrative.

The final three marks are secured with the third citation and its explanation. It identifies an important moment of suspense and thrill, and the explanation accurately describes how this situational high point generates excitement and apprehension.

All chosen examples for this question showcase a clear understanding of the literary techniques used in the text to build thrill and tension. Furthermore, the answers also demonstrate a comprehension of how specific phrases and sentences contribute to making a piece of writing more thrilling for the reader.

Paper Three

In this passage, Chuck Havers, a lowly character who maintains and lives in an oversized theme park, started a peculiar activity that made him the laughing stock of his community. Motivated by the hopeful belief that treasures may be hidden in the mundane, Chuck took on the task of meticulously sorting through the trash discarded by guests in an attempt to find something of value.

***

Like some lumbering woolly mammoth with a sack, Chuck moved slowly and deliberately, zig-zagging through the sea of plastic trinkets, unwanted popcorn bags, and dodgy cotton candy wrappers. He'd bow low to deposit things into his massive bag, contorting himself at odd angles to reach the bits wedged in unseen crevices.

"Havers's gone bye-bye," whispered Rick among the crew, giggles echoing in troth. Derision was the day's seasoning, vinegar to the salted fries of amusement park life.

Chuck endured, steadfast in his piety to the lost and discarded. He believed, more than religious zealotry could ever afford, in the idea of looking in the unlikeliest of places for those unheralded treasures. "Not every man's trash," Chuck murmured, clutching an orphan carousel ticket, "need be another man's trash as well".

The town jeered him, fair-weather friends voted him mad and voices on the park radio crackled in crude imitation. Everyone loved a circus, and Chuck had volunteered to be the clown; yet, he clung desperately to the faith that shaped his narrative, dismissing the snarling laughs as candied distractions.

One day, in the silent effulgence of a receding summer dusk, Chuck's bag felt a bit heavier. Not the weary weight of accumulated trash, but a profound heft that pulled at him. Pausing midway through the littered funfair maze, his gloved hand dove into the dark recesses of his sack. It emerged, glittering against the twilight, clasping a beautiful gold pocket watch.

The run-down, forsaken timepiece bore the craftsmanship of antiquity, its once-overlooked grandeur crippled by time and negligence. Chuck, revering it as an artifact, marveled at the intricate motifs inscribed on the seemingly gold façade. It was his vindication, his Holy Grail— a keystone to defend his belief, his hope.

Word soon snaked through the small community, weaving a miraculous tale tale of a pauper turning prince. Skepticism-ripped faces now taut with remorse, sentences spun in wild fervors of regret. Among the din of excitement, persisted the quiet triumph of Chuck Havers.

Leaning against the still Circle-o-Ride, looking to the descending moon with glittery eyes, he muttered, "It was never about the garbage, not once," raising his treasure to the celestial bodies, "but the stories they carried."

Extract from 'The Jester's Jewels' by Thomas R. Eddison.

QUESTIONS

1. Put the following events in the order in which they occur in the extract. Number them from one to five, where one happens first and five happens last. [5]

The community begins to view Chuck in a new light. ☐

Chuck finds a gold pocket watch. ☐

Rick and his fellow crew members mock Chuck. ☐

Chuck's former critics express regret for doubting him. ☐

Chuck sifts through discarded items at the amusement park. ☐

2. Consider paragraph four. How does Chuck likely feel in reaction to the negative attitudes of those around him? Use your own words and evidence from the text. [4]

_____
_____
_____
_____
_____
_____
_____
_____

3. The author uses the following simile in the first paragraph: "Like some lumbering woolly mammoth with a sack, Chuck moved slowly and deliberately." What kind of impression does this create in your mind? [4]

_____
_____
_____
_____

4. What might Chuck be meaning when he says, "It was never about the garbage, not once... but the stories they carried." (paragraph 8)? [4]

5. Select the word or phrase that has the closest meaning to 'effulgence' (paragraph 5) from the following options. [2]

Dimness

Shimmer

Brightness

Roughness

Deafening

6. Look at paragraph two. Discuss how the writer creates an atmosphere of mockery and amusement. Include two specific examples from the paragraph in your answer. [4]

_____
_____
_____
_____

7. In your own words, explain what happens when Chuck finds the gold pocket watch. [4]

8. **Think of two words that, in your opinion, best describe Chuck's change in status within his community. [4]**

Word 1:

Word 2:

_____
_____

9. Identify three points in the passage where the author injects suspense into the narrative. For each example, write the paragraph number and explain how the author makes the moment suspenseful or engaging. [9]

Example:

_____
_____

Explanation:

_____
_____
_____
_____

Example:

_____
_____

Explanation:

_____
_____
_____
_____

Example:

_____

_____

Explanation:

_____

_____

_____

_____

MODEL ANSWERS

1. Put the following events in the order in which they occur in the extract. Number them from one to five, where one happens first and five happens last. [5]

The order of events is as follows:

1) Chuck sifts through discarded items at the amusement park.

2) Rick and his fellow crew members mock Chuck.

3) Chuck finds a gold pocket watch.

4) The community begins to view Chuck in a new light.

5) Chuck's former critics express regret for doubting him.

2. Consider paragraph four. How does Chuck likely feel in reaction to the negative attitudes of those around him? Use your own words and evidence from the text. [4]

Despite enduring the cruel mockery from his community, Chuck remains undeterred and, in a way, defiant. He brushes off the scorn and laughter as "candied distractions", suggesting his ability to stay focussed on his belief and mission. He clings to his faith, hinting at a stoic resilience. This tenacity shows that while the derision may sting, it fails to break his resolve. The derision of others does not deter him, instead, it appears to strengthen his conviction in his peculiar endeavour.

3. The author uses the following simile in the first paragraph: "Like some lumbering woolly mammoth with a sack, Chuck moved slowly and deliberately." What kind of impression does this create in your mind? [4]

The simile portrays Chuck as a massive, methodical, and determined creature, reminiscent of a woolly mammoth. The deliberate comparison to the prehistoric beast indicates Chuck's detachment from the fast-paced, modern world around him. It also illustrates his dogged dedication and slow, systematic approach to sifting through the discarded items. This simile furthermore adds a touch of the surreal and whimsical to Chuck's endeavour, underlining the peculiar and eye-catching nature of his task amid a theme park strewn with garbage.

4. What might Chuck be meaning when he says, "It was never about the garbage, not once... but the stories they carried." (paragraph 8)? [4]

Here, Chuck states that his pursuit was never about the physical trash he was picking, but rather the history and stories that the discarded items encapsulate. He is effectively saying that these rubbish items carry within them experiences and narratives that are often overlooked but nonetheless valuable. As such, the actual physical items are just the tangible manifestation of these stories - the truly worthwhile element is the narrative and human experience each item holds.

5. Select the phrase that has the closest meaning to 'effulgence' (paragraph 5) from the following options. [2]

Dimness

Shimmer

Brightness

Roughness

Deafening

The word with the closest meaning to 'effulgence' is 'brightness'.

6. Look at paragraph two. Discuss how the writer creates an atmosphere of mockery and amusement. Include two specific examples from the paragraph in your answer. [4]

In paragraph two, the author skillfully uses language to craft an atmosphere filled with mockery and humour. Firstly, the author employs dialogue to directly express derision with phrases like "Havers's gone bye-bye". The casual, almost childlike language heightens the feeling of ridicule and reduces Chuck's effort to a childish antic in the eyes of his peers. Secondly, the author uses an interesting gastronomical metaphor – "Derision was the day's seasoning, vinegar to the salted fries of amusement park life" – to further enhance the sense of casual mockery. The metaphor suggests that mocking Chuck adds a sort of flavour or entertainment value to the otherwise monotonous and repetitive amusement park life, thereby establishing an atmosphere of humour amongst the crew.

7. In your own words, explain what happens when Chuck finds the gold pocket watch. [4]

One evening, while Chuck sifts through the park's debris as usual, something feels different. His usual load, packed with bits and pieces of discarded knick-knacks, has an unusual heaviness. Amid the mess, his gloved hand pulls out a discarded, forgotten gold pocket watch. Its intricate designs and an aura of antiquity catch his eye. This discovery feels momentous to Chuck, a justification of his faith in the treasures hidden in the seemingly ordinary. In his eyes, it transforms instantly from a lost artifact to a symbol of his vindication.

* * *

8. Think of two words that, in your opinion, best describe Chuck's change in status within his community. [4]

Word 1: Transformed: Chuck's status within his community went through a total change following the discovery of the gold pocket watch. Before, he was seen as a laughingstock or a madman, but after, he becomes someone of interest, with a sort of newfound respect from his peers.

Word 2: Redeemed: Chuck's actions had previously caused his peers to doubt his sanity, but after proving the value in his explored belief, he earns back any lost respect and grace, hence redeeming his persona in the eyes of his community.

* * *

9. Identify three points in the passage where the author injects suspense into the narrative. For each example, write the paragraph number and explain how the author makes the moment suspenseful or engaging. [9]

Point 1: Paragraph 1: In this paragraph, we see Chuck moving with purpose, digging through mountains of seemingly irrelevant items.

Explanation: This section creates suspense by making us wonder what he could possibly find amongst such ordinary things. With phrases like "slowly and deliberately zig-zagging" and "contorting himself at odd angles", we are painted a picture of a man hell-bent on his pursuit, leaving us both curious and excited about the fruits of such determined exertions.

Point 2: Paragraph 5: The suspense heightens when Chuck's bag feels unusually heavy.

Explanation: Extravagant descriptions like "silent effulgence" and "profound heft" make us wonder about the mysterious object causing that unique weight, hence heightening the suspense. The author contrasts the usual "weary weight" of his load with a "profound heft" to heighten the anticipation – an anticipation that culminates with Chuck's plunge into the "dark recesses" of his bag in search of the item causing the unexpected change.

Point 3: Paragraph 8: The moment when Chuck comments on the real meaning of his endeavour provides another kind of suspense.

Explanation: This vignettes creates suspense because readers are left wondering what exciting tales are hidden behind the found items and what future stories they may create. The description of him "looking to the descending moon" and observing "his treasure to the celestial bodies," sets a dramatic and suspenseful stage, as we are left in wonderment about the profound and enlightening story behind the seemingly mundane "garbage." His revelation about the "stories" carried by the items underlines the ongoing suspense – and sparks anticipation about potential future miraculous finds.

Commentary on Model Answers

Question 1

This answer successfully replicates the chronological sequence of events as they unfold in the extract. Each mark is scored for correctly placing each individual event in its correct place. So, for example, the first correct spot - 'Chuck sifts through discarded items at the amusement park' – earns one mark, the second - 'Rick and his fellow crew members mock Chuck' – earns the second mark, and so on. Meticulously reading the extract and accurately replicating the order of events in relation to what is specifically asked is key to grabbing all the marks in a sequence-based question like this. Different shades of meaning could be taken from the phrasing of the events, so the precise arrangement of events might vary, however the answer offers a logical interpretation.

Question 2

The first mark is earned for correctly identifying that Chuck feels defiant against the mocking from his community. This demonstrates comprehension of the subtler emotional details of the extract. The second mark is earned for insightfully recognising that the abuse actually strengthens his resolve, providing an in-depth analysis of Chuck's response. The third mark is achieved by extracting the phrase 'candied distractions' and highlighting its relevance to the understanding of Chuck's feelings. The fourth mark is scored by recognising the severity of the abuse – 'stoic resilience' – and hence, delving deeper into Chuck's emotional strength. An alternative approach could be to discuss slightly more the external mockery, and how it contrasts with Chuck's internal steadfastness.

Question 3

The first mark is secured by extrapolating the characteristics embodied by the woolly mammoth simile. The model answer perceptively links the mammoth to Chuck's massive presence, methodical nature, and determined approach, providing depth to the image it conjures. The second mark is achieved by contextualizing the simile within the story's framework. The mention of Chuck's detachment from the fast-paced, modern world, as illustrated by the mammoth, showcases an understanding of how the author employs the simile to comment on Chuck's unique place within his surroundings. The third mark is clinched through an examination of the implications of the simile. By pointing out Chuck's systematic way of sifting through discarded items, the model answer captures the sense of dedication and single-mindedness driving Chuck's actions. Lastly, the fourth mark is credited to recognizing the surreal, whimsical quality the simile imparts to the scene. By emphasizing the peculiarity of Chuck's task within a theme park, the model answer captures the juxtaposition of the old-world mammoth amidst a modern-day setting, reinforcing the contrast and intrigue in the narrative. Another approach that could have been taken to earn marks would be to further dissect the words 'lumbering' and 'mammoth' from the simile. Analyzing 'lumbering' could hint at Chuck's possible clumsy or cumbersome appearance, while focusing on 'mammoth' might suggest a sense of him feeling out of place or archaic within the modern theme park. Such an approach would offer a more nuanced understanding of the simile's layered significance.

Question 4

In this answer, the first mark is earned by correctly interpreting Chuck's phrase to mean that the physical items of trash were not as important as the stories they told. The second mark is achieved for recognising that Chuck sees these discarded items as being linked with human experiences and personal narratives. The third mark is scored for indicating that these experiences have often been overlooked, hinting at the broader social commentary in the extract. The fourth mark comes from recognising that these items are merely manifestations of the more valuable entities – the stories they carry. An alternative interpretation could have been to emphasise more the perspective of 'value' and 'worth', that is, trash to one could be a treasure to another.

Question 5

Question five is a vocabulary-based question. In this case, you simply needed to correctly identify the meaning of 'effulgence'. The answer correctly identifies 'effulgence' to mean 'brightness', thus gaining full marks. It's worth noting that understanding the text's context, and the overall mood and tone it has set can help to logically deduce which option fits best, if you are unsure of what the word means exactly.

Question 6

The first mark is gained by identifying the use of dialogue to help convey the atmosphere of mockery. Another approach could have been to mention the juvenile language used, like 'bye-bye', when referring to the adult Chuck, which infantilises and belittles him. The second mark is scored for identifying the metaphor about derision being a seasoning, which reinforces the prevalent mockery. The third mark is won for interpreting the metaphor in the context of the mocking atmosphere, demonstrating an understanding of how the metaphor fits into the overall atmosphere of the extract. The fourth mark comes from indicating how the metaphor transforms the mockery from being a negative aspect into an entertaining diversion for the other characters, thus deepening our understanding of their derision towards Chuck. Another possible approach would be to discuss the use of the phrasing 'vinegar to the salted fries of amusement park life', as a tool to turn casual jeering into a staple of life in the amusement park.

Question 7:

The first mark is earned by noting that something felt different about Chuck's bag on the day he discovered the pocket watch. This introduces a turning point, showcasing an understanding of how the narrative shift s.

The second mark is awarded for successfully describing what Chuck locates

- the gold pocket watch, marking the culmination of his incessant trash picking habit.

The third mark is achieved by recognising the significance of the pocket watch from Chuck's perspective: the beautiful craftsmanship attributed an aura of antiquity to it, offering reasons why Chuck considered it a find of significant value.

The fourth mark comes from noting that the discovery is a 'vindication' for Chuck. This recognises and appreciates Chuck's perspective - his conviction in the possibility of finding value in what others disregard.

Question 8:

The first mark comes from making a thoughtful choice of the word "Transformed". It accurately describes the complete change in how the community perceives Chuck following his remarkable discovery.

The second mark comes from the second choice, "Redeemed", conveying the idea that Chuck has regained respect and validation from the community.

Justifying each choice by referring back to the text, reinforces these choices and demonstrates a comprehension of the themes and nuances of the story.

Question 9:

The first three marks come from the first instance of suspense. Mark one comes from correctly identifying an instance of suspense – Chuck's meticulous efforts in digging through waste. The recount of the particular action together with direct evidence from the paragraph make up the other two marks.

The next three marks comes from the second instance of suspense indicated. Mark one comes from correctly identifying the unexpected heaviness of the bag as a suspenseful element. The ensuing explanation, supported by textual evidence, earns the remaining two marks.

The final three marks come from recognizing Chuck's reflection on his actions as the third instance of suspense. The first mark comes from correctly identifying this retrospective instance. The explanation defending this choice, backed with textual references, earns the remaining two marks.

Here, the understanding of suspense doesn't remain limited to dramatic or thrilling events. The acknowledgement of less tangible moments of anticipation, like reflections and turning points in a narrative, showcase a deeper understanding of the text and the writer's intent.

Paper Four

In a small rural town, young Tom Bartley has decided to personally sabotage any attempts by the town barber to give him his usual summer cut.

***

The morning was bright and fragrant with the smell of honeysuckles, but Tom Bartley had more pressing matters at hand than enjoying the summer foliage. Tom feared the annual ritual of a dreaded summer haircut - a humiliation he was determined to thwart at all costs. He'd assembled an elaborate diversion involving a mouldy carp, five Cornish hens and the local constable's hat, a plan so whimsical it could only have been conceived by a ten-year-old.

He started by strategically placing the carp in sweet old Mrs. Humbert's mail slot. When she walked out to collect her letters and discovered the scented surprise, a wail echoed across the town that very well woke the dead.

Meanwhile, Tom liberated the five plump hens from fat-cheeked Delilah's poultry yard, setting them loose in the town square where they squawked, fluttered and flapped like chickens gone mad. This caused such chaos as town folks stumbled across this poultry pandemonium. Even grumpy old Dan, the blacksmith, was seen rolling about on the ground, swiping his large hands in the air in a vain attempt to catch one of the feathered fiends.

With the town thus distracted, Tom took his last precaution - he removed the impressive tall hat from the head of the absent-minded constable, adding a layer of chicken feed to the brim before replacing it. As the constable began to chase after the hens, their attraction to his hat turned the chase into a spectacle that drew eyes, and laughter, from everyone in attendance.

Tom expected that in all this confusion he could comfortably avoid his imminent haircut. The town's barber, big-handed Bert, would hopefully be too busy laughing or helping chase wayward hens to remember his set appointment. Yet this is where Tom miscalculated. Bert always kept his appointments on his wrist watch, a keepsake from his granddad, and even in the midst of poultry-induced chaos, he'd noticed Tom hiding behind the water well.

Before Tom knew it, he was seated in the barber's chair, his wild mane being tamed under Bert's confident ministrations. The town was still in shambles outside, with chickens squawking and old ladies screaming, but Bert was a man of habit. And Tom found, despite his clever efforts, his beautiful hair was still cascading down onto Bert's floor. However, he did notice that Bert was laughing so hard at the chaos in town square that some of his hair was left a little longer than usual.

By afternoon, the distraction had been mollified - the carp discarded, the hens recaptured, and the constable's hat de-crumbed. Little did the town know, it was young Tom who'd orchestrated the turbulent morning. As he walked home, his head a bit lighter and his face flamed with embarrassment, there was a small glimmer of triumph in his eyes.

"If a man does not find something he will die for, he isn't fit to live," he told his dog, Toby.

And although Toby, being a dog, did not understand English, he was more than happy to lick the remaining chicken feed off Tom's fingers, tails wagging and eyes filled with the type of simple, unconditional love that makes one feel like the most important person in the world.

Extract from The Haircut Hullabaloo by Mark K. Finn.

13+ Comprehension

QUESTIONS

1) List these five events in the order they occur in the extract. [5 marks]

- Tom Bartley finds himself in the barber's chair.
- Tom Bartley places a mouldy carp in Mrs. Humbert's mail slot.
- Local constable starts chasing loose hens.
- Tom Bartley sets loose hens in the town square.
- The barber notices Tom Bartley hiding.

☐
☐
☐
☐
☐

2) Look at paragraph 7. Using your own words, describe Tom Bartley's feelings as he walks home after the event. [4 marks]

_____
_____
_____
_____
_____
_____
_____

3) Take a look at the metaphor in paragraph 2: 'a wail echoed across the town that very well woke the dead.' What does this metaphor make you imagine? [4 marks]

_____
_____
_____

4) Explain what you think is meant by the phrase, "If a man does not find something he will die for, he isn't fit to live" in paragraph 8. [4 marks]

5) Choose the closest meaning to the word 'ministrations' (paragraph 9). Circle the correct answer. [2 marks]

a) Distractions
b) Annoyances
c) Services
d) Interruptions.

6) Look at paragraph 6 and explain how the author builds a comical atmosphere in this part of the extract. Make sure to include two quotes to support your answer. [4 marks]

_____
_____
_____
_____
_____
_____
_____
_____

7) In your own words, explain how Tom Bartley's plan to avoid his haircut unfolded and created a messy situation in town. [4 marks]

_____
_____
_____
_____
_____
_____
_____
_____

8) Think of two words to describe Tom Bartley's plan to avoid his haircut. [4 marks]

8a.

_____
_____

8b.

_____
_____

9) Look back at the entire extract and find three points where the author adds excitement to the story. For each point, provide the paragraph number and explain why you find it exciting. [9 marks]

Example:

_____
_____

Explanation:

_____
_____
_____
_____

Example:

Explanation:

Example:

Explanation:

MODEL ANSWERS

1) List these five events in the order they occur in the extract. [5 marks]

Arranged in the order they occur in the extract, the events are as follows:

1) Tom Bartley places a mouldy carp in Mrs. Humbert's mail slot.

2) Tom Bartley sets loose hens in the town square.

3) Local constable starts chasing loose hens.

4) The barber notices Tom Bartley hiding.

5) Tom Bartley finds himself in the barber's chair.

2) Look at paragraph 7. Using your own words, describe Tom Bartley's feelings as he walks home after the event. [4 marks]

Tom Bartley, while feeling both embarrassed by his conspicuous hair cut and disappointed by his unsuccessful efforts to avert it, also experiences a sense of accomplishment. Despite the botched plot, Tom takes solace in the disruption he's caused, managing to retain a shred of his intended rebellion. His emotions are mixed yet, against the odds, a tiny glimmer of triumph still sparkles in his eyes, revealing his pride in his audacious, albeit futile, mission.

3) Take a look at the metaphor in paragraph 2: 'a wail echoed across the town that very well woke the dead.' What does this metaphor make you imagine? [4 marks]

The metaphor 'a wail echoed across the town that very well woke the dead' paints a vivid, evocative picture of Mrs. Humbert's reaction. It suggests not just an ordinary cry, but one that is so intense and all-encompassing that its reach could theoretically extend beyond the boundaries of life, disturbing the tranquil repose of the departed. Such a metaphor heightens the drama of the scene, underscoring the unexpected and jarring nature of Tom's prank on the unsuspecting Mrs. Humbert. By likening the outcry to something that could awaken the deceased, the author is inviting us, the readers, to imagine the sheer volume and emotional weight of that outcry. Furthermore, it conveys the town's close-knit nature, wherein a single event can ripple out, affecting everyone, almost as if the town itself is a singular, collective entity. It provides both a sense of hyperbole, magnifying the audacity of Tom's actions, and adds a layer of humour, showcasing the exaggerated consequences of a child's whimsical mischief.

4) Explain what you think is meant by the phrase, "If a man does not find something he will die for, he isn't fit to live" in paragraph 8. [4 marks]

This phrase conveys the idea that finding a purpose or a passion that one feels strongly about – one that you would metaphorically (or even literally) be willing to risk your life for – is an essential component of a fulfilling existence. In the context of the story, this phrase humorously reflects Tom's exaggerated commitment to maintaining his hair length, equating it to a cause worth fighting for.

5) Choose the closest meaning to the word 'ministrations' (paragraph 9). Circle the correct answer. [2 marks]

The closest meaning to the word 'ministrations' is (c) Services.

13+ Comprehension

6)Look at paragraph 6 and explain how the author builds a comical atmosphere in this part of the extract. Make sure to include two quotes to support your answer. [4 marks]

The author creates a comical atmosphere by describing the absurdity and slapstick-like nature of the chaos. The phrase 'chickens gone mad' captures the comedic absurdity of a usually quiet town being disrupted by barnyard animals. The image of 'grumpy old Dan...swiping his large hands in the air' illustrates a sudden, exaggerated, and almost cartoonish scene of a powerful man desperately struggling to catch a chicken, which adds a further humorous touch. Through such imagery, the author provides an atmosphere of light-hearted mischief and hilarity.

7) In your own words, explain how Tom Bartley's plan to avoid his haircut unfolded and created a messy situation in the town. [4 marks]

Tom Bartley's cunning plan to avoid his summer haircut began with him planting a foul-smelling, mouldy carp in Mrs. Humbert's mail slot. Upon discovering the odorous carp, she let out a scream that resonated throughout the town. Concurrently, Tom released five Cornish hens from Delilah's poultry yard into the town square which led to a comic spectacle as townsfolk unwittingly became involved in corralling the confused hens. Adding more chaos to the situation, Tom manipulated the town constable into becoming a target for the hens by sprinkling chicken feed into his hat. The constable's chase aft er the hens caused even more confusion, making the entire town square a scene of hilarious disturbance. Tom hoped that amid this confusion, he could sneak away from his haircut appointment. However, despite the town being in chaos, the barber managed to catch Tom out.

8) Think of two words to describe Tom Bartley's plan to avoid his haircut. [4 marks]

8a. Ingenious: Tom's plan involves elements of surprise, diversion, and a good understanding of the townspeople's behaviour. It shows the strong imaginative and problem-solving skills of a ten-year-old trying to avoid a haircut.

8b. Chaotic: Even though Tom's plan was clever, it created an enormous mess in the town. The result was a pandemonium involving hens running loose, old ladies screaming, and the constable essentially wearing a hat of chicken feed.

9) Look back at the entire extract and find three points where the author adds excitement to the story. For each point, provide the paragraph number and explain why you find it exciting. [9 marks]

Example 1: Paragraph 2: Tom places the carp in Mrs Humbert's mailslot.

Explanation: This initial mischievous act, with Tom 'strategically placing the carp in sweet old Mrs. Humbert's mail slot,' serves as the catalyst for the entire sequence of events that follow. The specific choice of the word 'strategically' infers an intricate plan, pulling readers into a palpable suspense. We are left on tenterhooks, pondering not just Mrs. Humbert's impending reaction, but the potential domino effect this action might have in exposing Tom's entire ruse

Example 2: Paragraph 3: Tom releases the hens.

As Tom 'liberated the five plump hens from fat-cheeked Delilah's poultry yard,' there's an immediate escalation of chaos and disorder. The act of releasing these hens - and their subsequent antics as 'chickens gone mad' - paints a picture of hilarious anarchy. Finn's language choice, particularly with the image of 'poultry pandemonium' and a blacksmith 'rolling about on the ground', does more than just describe a scene; it masterfully immerses readers into the very heart of the commotion, allowing them to feel the sheer, almost tangible excitement and frenzy of the moment.

Example 3: Paragraph 5: Barber catches Tom.

In an ironic turn of events, after all of Tom's intricate planning and diversion tactics, Bert the barber, anchored by the importance of his "wrist watch, a keepsake from his granddad," spots Tom "hiding behind the water well". This revelation is thrilling because it's unexpected. After witnessing Tom's carefully orchestrated chaos, readers are lulled into thinking he might succeed in avoiding his haircut. However, Finn brilliantly subverts these expectations, demonstrating that even the most elaborate plans can be undone by something as simple and steadfast as a barber's routine. This twist re-emphasises the theme of childhood versus adult responsibilities and adds a layer of poignant excitement as we realise Tom's rebellious adventure might be futile after all.

Commentary on Model Answers

Question 1

The first mark for question 1 is gained by correctly identifying the first event in the extract, which is 'Tom Bartley places a mouldy carp in Mrs. Humbert's mail slot'. The second mark is earned by identifying the next event correctly as 'Tom Bartley sets loose hens in the town square'. The third mark is awarded by recognising 'Local constable starts chasing loose hens' as the third event. The fourth and fifth marks are achieved by correctly placing 'The barber notices Tom Bartley hiding and calls him in' and 'Tom Bartley finds himself in the barber's chair' as the fourth and fifth events respectively. This sequencing of the events accurately reflects their occurrence in the extract. A common possible confusion might have been the sequence of the constable chasing the hens and the barber noticing Tom, but careful reading provides the accurate sequence.

Question 2

The first mark of question 2 is secured by interpreting Tom's feeling of 'embarrassment' correctly. The second mark is attained by acknowledging Tom's feeling of 'disappointment' over his plot's failure. The third mark is earned by picking up on the faint thread of 'accomplishment' that Tom feels. And, the fourth mark is achieved through capturing the small 'glimmer of triumph' in Tom's eyes. There could be various interpretation to Tom's feelings at this point but the key is to draw inferences from the text to ensure accurate and plausible responses.

Question 3

For question 3, the opening of the response immediately secures the first mark by elucidating the metaphor's vivid portrayal of Mrs. Humbert's reaction, emphasising its overwhelming intensity. The second mark is garnered by delving deeper into the metaphor's implications, suggesting it goes beyond mere volume, hinting at an emotional depth that could transcend the barriers of life and death. A third mark is obtained by highlighting the dramatic role the metaphor plays in the narrative, not only stressing the surprise element of Tom's prank but also the broader repercussions it had on the community. Finally, the fourth mark is achieved through a layered analysis that brings out the hyperbolic nature of the metaphor and its humorous undertone, while also pointing to the interconnectedness of the town's inhabitants and their collective experience of events.

Question 4

The first mark of question 4 is achieved by understanding the phrase "If a man does not find something he will die for, he isn't fit to live" in literal terms, as relating to finding a purpose or passion. The second mark comes from the extension of this explanation: the willingness to risk your life for the cause you believe in. The third mark is for contextualising the phrase within the story, indicating it humorously reflects Tom's determination to avoid the haircut above everything else. Finally, the fourth mark is achieved by linking this quotation back to the character of Tom himself reinforcing his characterisation.

Question 5

The mark for question 5 is awarded for correctly identifying the synonym of 'ministrations'. Here, the correct answer is 'Services'. One way of approaching this question would be to look at the context in which the word is used in the passage instead of simply trying to recollect a synonym or decipher the word's meaning.

Question 6

The first mark for question 6 comes from correctly referencing the phrase 'chickens gone mad'. The second and third marks are given for citing 'grumpy old Dan...swiping his large hands in the air' and interpreting it as an indication of the humour in the text. The fourth mark is gained by explaining how this imagery, along with the presentation of the town's unusual and chaotic scene, builds a comedic and light-hearted atmosphere in the text. A different approach here could have been to focus also on the characterisation of grumpy old Dan and how his actions add more to the comical effect.

Question 7:

In this response, we start by explaining the steps Tom went through to sabotage his haircut appointment. The key elements of the plot, such as placing the mouldy carp and releasing the hens are highlighted first. This grabs one mark for understanding the key events. For the second mark, we highlight the novelty of Tom's plan, showing an understanding of the unique and amusing tools he used. The chaos caused by the released hens secures another mark, as we link the events to the broader impact on the town. The last mark is obtained by discussing the unexpected twist - despite the distracting chaos, Tom still ends up in the barber's chair.

Question 8:

The mark for this question is secured by the judicious selection of adjectives that accurately describe Tom's plan. 'Ingenious' and 'Chaotic' were chosen because they fully encompass the clever yet disorderly nature of Tom's plan. These words also align with the tone of the text - a balance between admiration for Tom's creativity, and amusement at the resulting disorder.

Question 9:

The answer for question 9 demonstrates a detailed understanding of the narrative's exciting moments, analyzed with precision and depth.

The first example from paragraph 3 captures the initiation of Tom's plan, securing the first three marks. The subsequent explanation highlights the suspense of this moment, referencing the specific term "strategically" to underscore Tom's careful plotting. This close reading and insight into the narrative ensures the acquisition of the fourth mark for this section.

Moving to the second example from paragraph 5, the answer identifies the heightened chaos brought on by the release of the hens, easily obtaining the next three marks. The explanation, by weaving in quotes like "chickens gone mad" and "poultry pandemonium", depicts the scene's comical tumult. This apt use of textual evidence and interpretation of the author's intent justifies the attainment of the fourth mark for this part.

The third example from paragraph 9 pinpoints the narrative's twist, earning three marks. The explanation delves into the significance of this event, contrasting Tom's mischief with the barber's discipline symbolized by his wristwatch. Recognizing the narrative tension in this moment ensures the securing of the fourth mark for this segment.

www.ingramcontent.com/pod-product-compliance
Lightning Source LLC
Chambersburg PA
CBHW081728100526
44591CB00016B/2542